The Crow Gods

Sarah Connor

Edited by Sarah Connor and Annick Yerem

SÍDHE PRESS

The Crow Gods
Sarah Connor

Edited by Sarah Connor and Annick Yerem

Published 2023 by Sídhe Press
https://Sídhe-press.eu

Cover Art by Mike Bryson
Logo Art by Aida Vainieri Özkara
Design by Jane Cornwell
www.janecornwell.co.uk

Also from Sídhe Press:

Our Own Coordinates
Poems About Dementia- An Anthology

For Aussie.

Yes.

Contents

An introduction

A study in four seasons, from root's sap to rook on wire, in wait,
this is the story of flames rising, blazing, taking flight, the wings of
those rooks, herrings, goldfinches growing, leaving, returning home,
all that flapping amid such balanced restraint, as much said in the
empty spaces, in all that's been given away, as there is in what's left
behind. This debut is a cacophony of life, the humming, fluttering,
chattering, glimmering, singing in cars and caravans crammed with
crumbs of former lives and loves, the purpose between the fear and
chaos. Here, Sarah Connor has captured the energy of the storm, the
taste of sunlight, the movement in the grass, the sharp edge of shadow
and sorrow against the tick tock of the wheel's turn. A significant
collection that's never anything less than sensory, Connor writes *That
bitch Courage never shows… none of us are brave… it's just that we
keep going.* If that's the case, Courage doesn't know the strength she's
missing. Extraordinary what a single bird can carry, how far the wing
can take us, the resilience of the beat within the breast. This might
be a first chapbook, but we are far from novice territory here. I've
bookmarked this into the memory.

Damien B Donnelly

Poet & producer

Being Human

This being human is all about telling stories,
it's travelling in a twisting caravan
across the desert, depending
on each other for flour,
for water, for a soft red blanket,
for bandages and apricots.

What currency do we have,
but stories? The story of "Good morning"
"How's this for weather?". The story of
"I love you", the story of childhood,
the story of how to stay safe,
how to eat well, how to survive
being lost, how to hold tight
to someone's hand.

It's whispering
our stories at night, the stories
of stars — of men, and beasts
and gods, and flaming suns.
It's singing our stories as we wash our plates,
as we wait for tea to brew,
as we clean our shoes.

It's shouting our stories in anger,

it's crooning them in love. It's sitting, silent,

round the campfire, listening.

We are stories, wrapped and tangled,

offered with love or fear or laughter.

This telling stories is all about being human.

Spring in the woods

Let's go to the woods. We should go now

because the woods are full of candles,

lit for a celebration. Small flames somehow

pushing up through thick soil, spangles

of red fire on dull brown twigs,

fat green candles, plump and swollen

gasping for life, waiting to be lit.

The woods are burning, green smoke rolling

over the hedgerows, just blurring those

sharp scratched winter lines. The woods are singing,

full of music. Don't ask me how I know.

I just know that we are candles, flinging

light across the space between us, light

that will burn and spread, flames that take flight.

Hare voice hare

Sometimes my voice is silent
the way a hare is still.

Again, my voice a hare
hidden in the long grass,
a hare quick-sprinting
up the field edge,
a hare darting
beneath a gate,

my voice suckling
my hidden children.

The rooks come home

Late evening,
when the sky's a paper lantern
lit by the tealight sun,
the rooks come home -

that low croak
of conversation. Of course,
they're sharing news -

new calves in the top field -
a fallen branch down by the stream -
that woman battling the wind
to get her washing in -
good lunching up the road -

moving from branch to branch,
like we might move around a room.

I left them

I left my children

in the care of birds –

in cities formed of twigs

and moss and down –

hoping they would be held

and safe. That they would

be fed. I hoped

they would grow beaks

and talons, and long, strong

feathers, that would give them flight.

Goldfinches

Stitching the hedge

to the sky

as if that

will keep the world

together

Is every bird

a needle?

It's hard

not to see joy

where we see

life

As far as we'll go

It's the middle of spring

and my mother is turning

into a bird. I'm a little afraid

that the wind up here

will blow her away

but she's smiling.

This is as far as we'll go.

The bench. The view.

The kids are roaming, aimless,

crushing the grass that's studded

with stitchwort and daisies, and

we walked here through cloud

after cloud of blackthorn, and bees,

but this is as far as we'll go.

We're high up here, and

sunshine in April

is always a blessing.

Lift up your face –

the sea is so blue,

and the waves are alive,

and everything's humming

and singing and fluttering –

but this as far as we'll go.

Peregrines

They are nesting in the tower again –
twin blades slicing heaven in two.
They wheel above us. We stand here,
point out their speed, their movement.

The hunter's eye makes out
a vole, a drift of pink rose petals,
a white veil blowing in the breeze,
a movement in the grass. A mouse.

Chicks wail for food. Somewhere below,
a baby reaches for a woman's hair,
protests as water splashes – cooler than rain.
A father swoops, kills, rises. A mother
praises him: his strength; his love.

Obby Oss

Masked, I'm mayhem, mischief,
I'm grab and run, I'm green shoots rising
I'm rain on dry soil

Masked, I'm spring and leaf
and blossom opening,
and the first sip of the bee

Masked, I'm silver herring
spilling and glimmering
across the quay

Masked, I'm ridden by the goddess,
and I ride her, until we're just
a roiling, rutting ball
of limbs and lust and dust and seed

Masked, I'm Jack o'the Green,
Jack in the Pulpit,
Jack the giant slayer

Unmasked, I'm Jack the lad,
outside the pub,
swilling a final pint,
spewing galaxies into the gutter

Sail

If I'm the mast, you are the sail -
I mean, the thing that drives us on -
letting the wind become momentum.

I thought the ocean was a barrier,
but you showed me it was connection,
and that the storms were energy –

but then again, I've held you -
tied you to all these things you love,
kept you from flying off too far,

losing too much. This is the power
we have together: to make purpose
out of fear and chaos. To keep moving.

Drizzle

Sunlight drizzled across the garden,

dripped from the plum tree,

puddled among the daisies.

The daffodils were drenched with it,

and it flooded under the door

and into the kitchen – leaving me

ankle deep in golden, pooling light -

unable, unwilling, to sweep it all away.

The swimmer

Rook slips into the air
like a child slipping
into water, trusting
that she will be held.
A current carries her
or, at least, she rides
the current, and rises,
circling, into the cold sky.

It's that first dip I love,
that drop, halted
by out-stretched wings –
fall, interrupted –

so brave, to trust
the emptiness.

Browse me

go on, then

browse me

flick your fingers through
my paper soul – underline
the words that quiver –
love lust hate

bookmark my memories

step from one image
to the next, unroll
a narrative

highlight the highlights
erase

bookmark my thoughts
write "yes, this!" in the margin
circle a pearl of wisdom
scrawl your name

Climbing the beech tree in your parents' garden

You will come to a place

where you can stop,

back pressed against the trunk -

a place where you can feel

your soft limbs branch and stiffen,

and the sap pulsing under

your skin; where all your thoughts

are nests and breezes,

and the taste of sunlight,

where the tree holds you,

like a father holds a child -

                Or maybe

your father hoists you up

onto his strong shoulders,

so you can peer through

the green leaves of his hair,

over the fence to where

next-door's cat lolls in the sunshine

and the old lady jabs

at her flowerbed

and now two butterflies

spiral up towards you

and a bird swoops in

to land upon a twig

and no-one else can see

the tree-ness of you.

Spirit

"There's red deer up on Thornhill Head" he says.

"They'll take a crop, a group like that. But beautiful".

He offers cider with a soil-stained paw.

"I've seen more hares the last two years. And hedgehogs.

Things are coming back. Red deer on Thornhill Head".

His eyes are very blue. He shakes his head.

"Now, starlings. They're a bugger. What a mess.

What can you do?". He leaves wide edges

on his fields, cuts hedges later than his father did.

He puts up boxes for the swifts. He smiles,

straddling the wild and the farmed, holding

it all in balance, in those spade-like hands.

Owned by the land, the ripe curves of it,

the steep-sided valleys, where the woods

shelter wild daffodils and bluebells,

and the gentler slopes for cattle and for maize.

You have to make a living. Then again,

you have to love this place. He smiles again.

"Red deer on Thornhill Head. That's wonderful".

The crow gods

First, I gave my hair,

because the gods are like crows.

My eyebrows and my lashes,

I gave them, too.

I gave my right breast

for the crow-gods to claw

and squabble over

with their cruel talons. My ovaries.

Great strips of skin I gave

to numbness. Three toenails, and

the feeling in my fingertips.

I gave my left breast

to be burnt: the crow-gods

love the smell of burning fat.

My hair grew back. I gave them that

again. A thumbnail.

Car

This car is full of ghosts – echoes of us,

trailing muddy boots, wet swimming costumes, snatched coffees.

Oh, we've lived here. Spilt water, secrets, fizzy drinks.

Shouted – at the radio, at the sat nav,

at each other. Told our stories of successes and betrayals.

We've slept here, heads lolling

on the long road north.

We'll clean it out before we sell it:

gather up old receipts for faded clothes,

stray Lego bricks and crumbs and seashells

that we gathered and forgot about.

Perhaps the future owner will still feel us

there – a waft of woodsmoke, or of chlorine,

or ice-cream's vanilla kiss. Perhaps

a giggle or a grumble from the back –

or perhaps the radio will play

an old Ed Sheeran song,

and we'll be there, singing along –

some of us out of key, or out of time –

still driving down these country roads

Silence

She stands in silence

holding an empty sign

because words have lost

all meaning now

words have become sounds,

the way a gull cries,

the way a fox barks in the night –

the way a bullet flies

the way a bomb falls

the way a boy cries

mum

mum

mum

Here

This is a stubborn place, I'd say.
Old names live on here. Bits of wild
cling to steep hillsides, linger
in forgotten corners.

Three nights ago, we saw a hare
lop-lollying along the ridges
in the maize field. I wonder
what she thinks of our machines,
our lines. We carve the landscape,
make divisions, demarcations.

Up on the hill, the farm name holds
the memory of a sacred grove.
Scrabbled scruffy stands of ash and oak
are still held sacred – never cut;
our hedgerows tangled sanctuaries –
blackthorn, hazel, haw –
small creatures hiding, homing there.

Last night an owl swooped silent

across Nick and Jennie's field,

clipping the long grass, almost.

We watched him scouting,

criss-crossing the scrubby corner

where the lane turns east.

Things are a little tatty here.

There's space for nesting sparrows,

jackdaws crank call from the bottom barn,

and the rooks nest all along

the field's top corner, and beyond.

You'll see them march

across the slurried fields.

They're after leatherjackets,

plunging beaks into the smelly ground.

Sometimes

we'll meet a deer, tip-toeing.

Wildness ebbs and flows –

a field left fallow,

a field ploughed,

an old hedge lost

to trees. A lane forgetting

it was ever paved.

We make accommodations here.

We let the nettles grow,

the brambles fling their skinny arms out.

We are not too fussy.

Well, we can't afford to be –

you turn your back round here

and the wild slips back,

whispering old stories,

old secrets, trailing

old scents, remembering.

Egg

My child sleeps, nested like an egg
smooth skinned and speckled,
full of the future.

My child curls, in the unheeded
sprawl of sheet, head covered
full of dreams.

My child is warmed by the softness
of feather and home, unblemished,
full of hope.

Solstice Storm

They bring the weather with them -
wild winds that flutter home-made pennants,
set lanterns rocking, shadows leaping
up canvas walls and wooden palisades -

they sing out loud, gathering in loose groups
and drinking sun-gold cider, moonlight vodka -
tell stories round the dancing flames
of midnight fires: their stories -
tales that shift and change
with every telling, forging their own myths.

They're gathering here before the solstice,
a ragged caravan of feathers, flapping, black;
of russet coats and cool green gazing;
of blues and yellows, splashing monochrome,
dark masks, striped faces, brown eyes
blinking in the light. A mustering of

muddy feet and velvet coats. Silk scarves
and dirty claws, and silver rings.

They bring the weather with them,

call up the wind, send cloud wolves

rioting across the sky,

wait for the sun to rise.

Lammastide

This time of year, the shadows
are the sharpest – cut by a blade –

stepping into the shade
is like stepping into church –

and all the world is dust and sweat,
so that you long for rain, knowing

that rain would ruin everything –
one storm tossed out of winter's pocket

would leave you hungry until spring.
What can you do? There's nothing, only

watch the skies. Make bread. And pray.

Postcard

Thank you

for the coastline

you sent me –

headlands reeling west,

land as wild

and joyful as a jig.

I'll stick it to

my fridge

and think of you,

and the sweet smell

of turf

Eavesdropping

Rook eavesdrops on our conversation,

a black shape, rising when he's heard the news,

dipping across the field, finding his gang -

and me, I eavesdrop on his chattering,

the calls from branch to branch,

wondering what news he shares,

what mockery, what love?

Fear and Courage

Fear grabs me in the bathroom -
kisses that leave me bruised and hurting -
I can still taste them now.

Fear texts me all the time,
drops postcards in the mail,
rings like a mad ex after midnight
won't stop calling me.

That bitch Courage never shows,
she never writes, she never phones,
it's like she doesn't know me.

None of us are brave.

It's just that we keep going,
one step, then another.

My son is teaching me to make a fire

Right here, where the little waves

lick and lap at the stones,

like kittens' tongues.

His hands are defter than I'd realised,

piling up twigs, and leaving space

so that the wind can whisper things to life,

and he can call sparks from a stone,

and nurture them, until the flames

are kittens' tongues themselves,

licking and lapping.

When we saw the chough at Lands End

Chattering stopped
as the bird skimmed its way
beneath our feet,
carving a path
between us and the sea

That beak a red flame –
that curved beak a blade
slicing through
the armour of the sky

Black feathers salted
by sea spray, cry echoing
across the Irish Sea

This bird, making itself
a gift to us, lighting a fire,
leaving us silenced.

The Green Clock

Samhain, and the nights draw in
and we move closer, stand together,
a little out of time, a little closer
to the edge of everything. Tick tock,
it's midnight, and we can only
hope the light will make its way to us,
this darkest, longest night - tick tock -
Imbolc - the first signs of spring,
pale snowdrops standing in the rain
and the fat buds of daffodils -
tick tock - the equinox - the world in balance

We stand on the edge
but how much leverage do we have?
We're the disruptors -
that's what humans do,
we tinker with our clever fingers,
fouling the mechanism. Tick tock.

Beltane, and the fires are lit
and lovers leap across the flames,
the heavy scent of mayflowers -
tick tock - and we hang suspended
in the light, right at the top
of the year's wheel and - tick tock -
Lughnasa and we start
our harvest, knead the first dough
of the first loaf, bite the first apple,
and we're rich and tick tock
equinox, and now we reap
what we have sown.

Samhain, and the nights draw in.
It's getting colder. Hold my hand.
Let's stand here, close together,
struggling by firelight,
trying to fix the mechanism,
fingers not so clever now,
each tiny wheel, each cog,
we scrabble for them.

Tick tock.

Writing a poem

The way a crow

curves its body

around its cry –

as if that cry

is something to be

hawked up

gobbed out

as if it hurts

the belly, scratches

the throat

but must escape

Oak

We forget the wisdom of the roots -

that strength that comes from plunging

into darkness. We forget

the way roots find their way,

questing for what they need.

We see the branches, and the leaves -

the glowing green of them,

the joyful dance. We see the acorns,

sitting snugly in their cups, the graceful

giving in to autumn. All that glory -

but the sap sinks deep into the roots,

lives out the winter. Waits for spring.

Roses

A response to Snow by Louis MacNeice

You came in, and suddenly
the room was full of roses,
as if you were the tipping point
that made it all make sense.

Inside, trapped warmth, rich scent,
and all those roses crawling up the walls,
across the curtains, and the glass vase
swelling on the wooden table,

one petal on the shiny surface, fallen.
Outside, winter, all lines and angles, woodcut.
The world turns in analogue, infinitesimal.,
but we see the moment when the load shifts.

World is evolution.

I'm struggling here. This room too
soft and fragrant. I could sink,
but there is something urgent
out there, beyond the glass.

Writing the wolf

I'm writing again

I'm writing a wolf.
I write that his coat gleams like ice
that his eyes shine like sunlight on snow

The wolf says "no".

I write his hunger. I write his belly
clenching against his spine,
his teeth biting down on air

No.

I write the scent of life
clinging to leaf and twig,
a red thread running
through a labyrinth

No.

I write the paw prints
ink on paper
the trail cutting away
to the horizon

Driving home

This road connects us
and divides us
and I drive it like
I'm on a quest

I drive it like
I'm cutting through
a hedge of thorns,
or like I'm climbing up
a mountain made of glass

I know each curve
each hill and yet
it's new each time
and I forget this bend,
this climb. I hate
the lorries that
crawl so slowly
and the tractors
I get stuck behind

because I'm driving

like I'm crossing

a great sea of ice,

or creeping through

a forest made of

sounds and shadows

and this road divides us

and connects us

so that I love it

and I hate it - waiting

for that moment

coming over the hill

when I see the moor

carved across the sky

and the tree that bends

away from the west wind

and the rook on the wire

and I'm home.

Acknowledgments

There are so many people who have had a hand in this! Anja has been a fantastic editor to work with, and Jane Cornwell has helped make this book look wonderful.

Mike Bryson – thank you for the crow. I love him. We love you, too. You left a hole in our lives, and we will always miss you.

Some of these poems have been midwived by other poets. The dVerse team – Bjorn Rudberg, Mary Grace Guevara, Victoria Ceretto-Slotto, De Jackson, Mish Beauchamp, Lillian Hallberg, Kim M Russell, Merril D Smith, Linda Lee Lyberg, Laura Bloomsbury, Frank J Tassone, Lisa Fox, Sanaa Rizvi, Ingrid Wilson, Punam Sharma – you are great people to work with, and great friends to have. Brendan from earthweal – thank you for giving me space to explore the year. Wendy Pratt – your workshops have been inspiring.

Thank you to Tanya Shadrick and Damien B Donnelly for their generous reading and words, and for their creation of spaces for expression. Thank you to Matt Smith for championing all our poetry. Thank you to Jane Dougherty for her early lessons in form and precision. I'm so glad I found you all.

Thank you to the people who make life more interesting and more fun. Aussie, Sadhbh, Fintan, Mum, Dad, Julian, Clare, Claire, Simon, Jane. All the PPVs.

Finally, the oncology team at RDUH, especially Dr Goodman, Dr Solomons, Dr Vijeratnam, Dr Carter. Without you, I quite literally wouldn't be here today.

Sarah Connor

Sarah Connor was brought up in South Yorkshire and now lives in North Devon. She spent her working life as a Child Psychiatrist. She has two adult children and one husband.

Sarah was diagnosed with breast cancer in 2008, and in 2012 discovered she had spread to her lungs and bones. She originally started blogging as a way of exploring her feelings about her diagnosis. When she began writing poetry she tried to keep these two worlds separate, but eventually realised that cancer invades everything.

Writing has enriched her life so much. She has been published in numerous publications, including Spelt magazine; The Storms; anthologies from Black Bough, Experiments in Literature and Sidhe Press. She is a regular writer of prompts at dVerse, and is still hanging about on Twitter. You can follow her there at @sacosw, and find her blogs at fmmewritespoems.wordpress.com and fantasticmetastaticme. wordpress.com.

Printed in Great Britain
by Amazon